This book belongs to

_____

This book is dedicated to my children - Mikey, Kobe, and Jojo.

Copyright © 2025 Grow Grit Press LLC. All rights reserved. No part of this book may be reproduced in any form without permission in writing from the publisher. Please send bulk order requests to info@ninjalifehacks.tv

Paperback ISBN: 979-8-89614-094-8
Hardcover ISBN: 979-8-89614-096-2
eBook ISBN: 979-8-89614-095-5

Printed and bound in the USA.
NinjaLifeHacks.tv

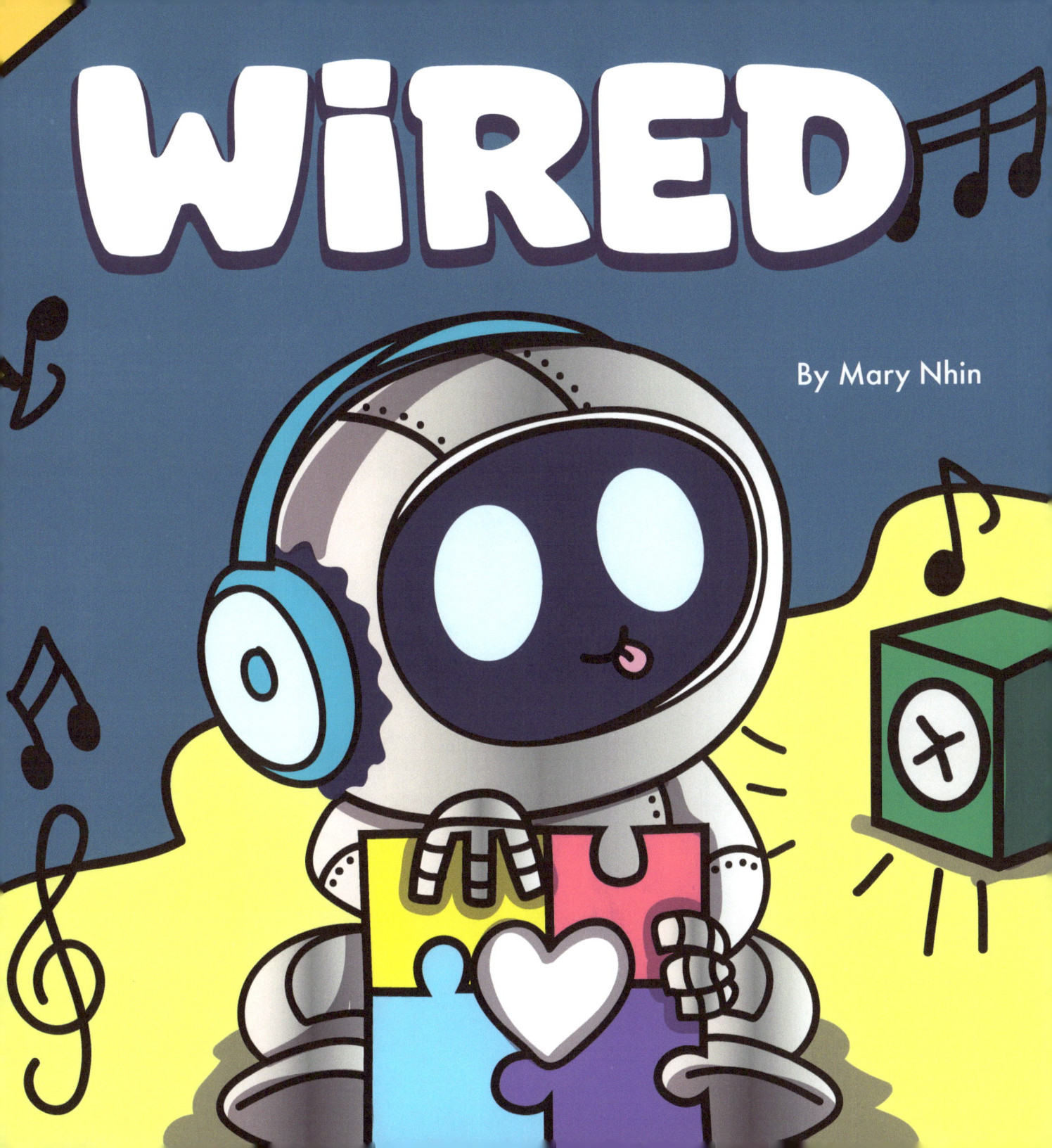

WiRED the robot had circuits so bright.
His brain buzzed and whirred from morning to night.
He *beeped* when excited, *booped* when unsure,
but sometimes the world felt *too much* to endure.

Tomorrow was Field Day, a big school event,
with races and games—it was *huge* what it meant!
But WiRED felt nervous—his circuits *buzzed tight*.
Would the noise and the changes feel way too *bright*?

"The whistles! The shouting! The blaring school bell!
The lunchroom's already *a sensory yell*!"
He covered his ears, his circuits on *high*,
"What if it's too much? What if I fry?!"

Then my buddy Chip rolled into sight,
with a happy beep and eyes so bright.
"I used to feel just like you do today,
but I use **T.U.N.E.** to help me send fears away!"

"First, **Take** a break when it all feels too loud.
Find a calm space, away from the crowd.
A quiet spot where I can reset,
and not short-circuit from all the stress yet!"

T - Take a Break

"Next, **use** your tools—so helpful, so smart!
Headphones, colored glasses, they all play a part.
A weighted vest helps my circuits feel tight,
so I don't get that 'floating in space' type of fright!"

U - Use Your Tools

"The buzzing, the beeping, the chaotic sound,
it rattles my system—it *spins me around*!
I **navigate** senses with hums or a tune,
a soft little song can make me immune!"

N - Navigate Senses

"And when plans go sideways or don't go as planned,
I **empower** myself to still take a stand!
A deep breath, a mantra—'I CAN BE BRAVE!'
No, I won't let it make me hide in a cave!"

E – Empower Myself

GO WIRED!

The next day was here, the big Field Day race.
WiRED took a breath and **set his own pace**.
When things got too loud, he knew what to do—
T.U.N.E. helped him power right through!

At the finish line, he stood tall and proud.
The noise and cheers were wild and loud.
But he grinned and he beamed—he didn't shut down.
WiRED *won the day,* no need for a frown!

Some people may say, "You're different, that's odd."
But different means *brilliant*, not something to nod!
I may not be wired like robots you see,
but my brain is amazing—it's perfect to me!

So when life feels tricky or overload's near,
I remember my T.U.N.E. and *face it with cheer*!
I'll **Take a break, Use my tools, Navigate, Empower,**
'cause neurodiverse minds grow stronger by the hour!

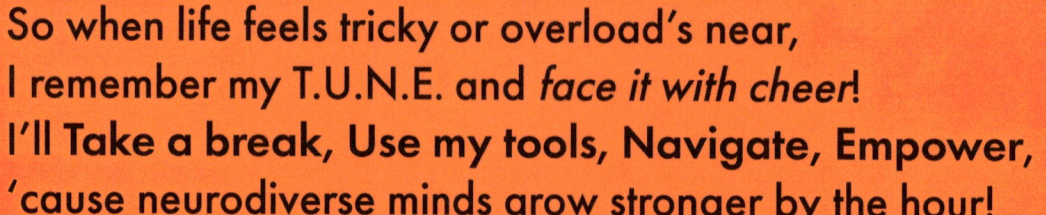

Check out our WiRED lesson plans that include fun activities!

I love to hear from my readers. Email me your feedback or thoughts on what my next story should be at info@ninjalifehacks.tv   Yours truly, Mary

 @marynhin   @GrowGrit
#NinjaLifeHacks

 Ninja Life Hacks

 Mary Nhin   Ninja Life Hacks

 @officialninjalifehacks

www.ingramcontent.com/pod-product-compliance
Lightning Source LLC
LaVergne TN
LVHW070436070526
838199LV00015B/527